FRANCE

GROLIER
EDUCATIONAL

Published 1999 by Grolier Educational
Sherman Turnpike, Danbury, Connecticut.
Copyright © 1999 Times Editions Pte Ltd. Singapore.

Set ISBN: 0-7172-9324-6
Volume ISBN: 0-7172-9331-9

CIP information available from the Library of Congress or the publisher

Brown Partworks Ltd.

Series Editor: Tessa Paul
Series Designer: Joyce Mason
Crafts devised and created by Susan Moxley
Music arrangements by Harry Boteler
Photographs by Bruce Mackie
Production: Alex Mackenzie
Stylists: Joyce Mason and Tessa Paul

For this volume:
Writer: Charles Phillips
Consultant: Carolyn Manyon
Editorial Assistants: Hannah Beardon and Paul Thompson

Printed in Italy

Adult supervision advised for all crafts and recipes,
particularly those involving sharp instruments and heat.

CONTENTS

FRANCE:

France lies on the western edge of Europe and is one of the largest countries on the continent. It has coastlines on the Mediterranean Sea, the Atlantic Ocean, and the English Channel.

English Channel

Dinan

Pont-Croix

River Loire

First Impressions

- **Population** 57,747,000
- **Largest city** Paris with a population of 9,318,821
- **Longest river** Loire
- **Highest mountain** Mont Blanc at 15,771 ft.
- **Exports** Machinery, vehicles, iron and steel, fruit, and wine
- **Capital city** Paris
- **Political status** Republic
- **Climate** Varies from wet and cool to hot and dry
- **Art and culture** France is famous as an artistic center. It also produces some of the finest wine in the world.

Atlantic Ocean

▶**The French countryside** is renowned for its elegant chateaux, or castles, surrounded by rolling hills. They were mostly built by the aristocracy, the rich rulers, of France before the French Revolution in 1789. Many chateaux have wonderful collections of art and furniture.

Lourdes

Spain

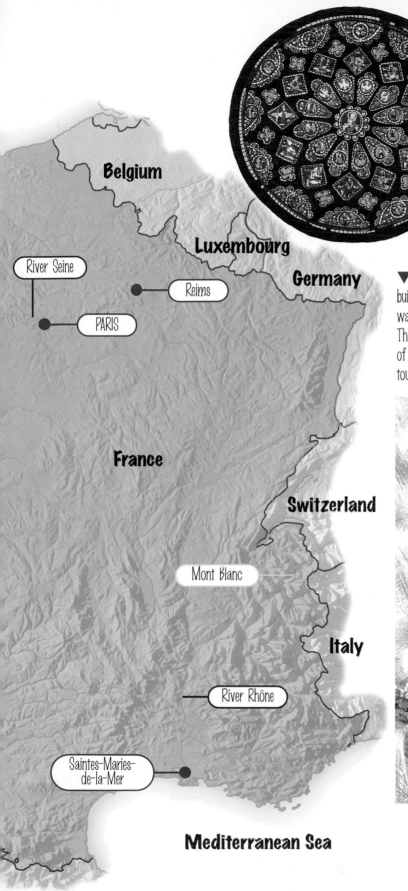

◀**Notre Dame Cathedral** in the town of Chartres is one of the finest in the world. It took only 30 years to build, which is a short time for a cathedral. It is famous for beautiful stained glass windows such as this rose window, which was made in the thirteenth century.

Belgium

Luxembourg

Germany

River Seine

Reims

PARIS

France

Switzerland

Mont Blanc

Italy

River Rhône

Saintes-Maries-de-la-Mer

Mediterranean Sea

▼**The Eiffel Tower** in Paris was built in 1889. It was built to celebrate the centenary of the French Revolution and was named after Gustav Eiffel, the man who designed it. The tower is made of iron and is 984 feet high. It is one of the world's most famous structures and is popular with tourists, who can take elevators all the way to the top.

RELIGIONS

Christianity is the main faith in France. In the 1500s and 1600s there was bitter conflict between groups in the church. At the time of the French Revolution the church came under attack for its support of the king. In modern France the church is separate from the state.

CHRISTIANITY reached the area of modern France in the second century A.D. Christians believe that Jesus Christ, who lived on earth 2,000 years ago, was the son of God. Catholics, who were loyal to the pope as head of the church, fought Protestants, who rejected the pope. After the king of France, Francis II, died in 1560 there was fighting in France for more than 30 years. One side was led by the Guise family, who were Catholics. The leaders of the other side were from the Bourbon family, who sided with the Protestants.

In 1586 the Catholic king Henry III was killed and a Protestant prince, Henry of Navarre, said he was now king. The people of Paris, however, were Catholics and would not let him into the city. He agreed to become a Catholic, but he issued a law in 1598 that French people were allowed to choose whether they wanted to be Catholic or Protestant. This law was changed in 1685, and many Protestants fled from France.

The church used its power to back up the French kings. In the 1620s and 1630s an important priest was also a chief minister to the king. When the French turned against their king in the French Revolution of 1789, the leaders of the revolution also turned against the church. In modern France the church and the state are separate.

French people are, of course, free to choose their faith nowadays. However, the majority are members of the Roman Catholic Church.

GREETINGS FROM **FRANCE!**

The French are proud of their language. For many years it was the tongue spoken by international diplomats, and it is the official language of 22 countries. In the eighteenth and nineteenth centuries France built up a number of colonies, countries dependent on and ruled by France. Some of these countries still use the French language. They include Congo and Senegal in Africa. In some countries, such as Canada, French is one of the official languages.

How do you say...

Hello
> **Bonjour**

How are you?
> **Comment ça va?**

My name is
> **Je m'appelle**

Goodbye
> **Au revoir**

Thank you
> **Merci**

Peace
> **La paix**

CARNAVAL

During Lent Christians recall the 40 days Jesus spent starving in the desert. They do so by giving up some pleasures during that time. Just before this dull Lenten period Christians enjoy parties, feasts, and carnivals.

One of the best carnivals in all France is the *Nice Carnaval*. Nice is a city in an area called Provence in the south of France.

For centuries the proud farmers of Provence showed off their fruit, vegetables, and flowers on special feast days. This old habit became a display of extravagance during the Carnaval in Nice. A tradition of throwing flowers also developed.

In the two weeks before Lent begins there are many street parades, but the "Battle of the Flowers" is the most famous. It takes place on the *Quai des Etats Unis* (USA Street). Girls parade on carriages pulled by horses. These girls throw thousands of flowers at the crowds who line the streets. They chuck the flowers back at the girls and their horses.

In the old days people used to throw flowers at each other all the time at Carnaval. However, in 1876 these "flower wars" were allowed their own day, and the "Battle of the Flowers" is now a major event at Nice Carnaval.

Menton is another town in Provence. Here, the farmers are very well known for their oranges and

Lemons and oranges grow well in southern France. In Menton the farmers display their rich crops during the feast days of Carnaval.

JOYEUSES PÂQUES

Lent ends at Easter. On the morning of Easter Sunday French people say to each other *"Joyeuses Pâques,"* or "Happy Easter." At Easter Christians celebrate Jesus's resurrection — how He rose to life again three days after dying. All through the week before Easter they think of the events leading up to Jesus's resurrection. On Maundy Thursday they remember His last supper, and on Good Friday they recall how He died on the cross. On Sunday Christ rose from the dead. Eggs and spring flowers represent new life. Christians make gifts of these on Easter Sunday.

Mimosa (above), irises (far left) and lilies (bottom) bloom in Nice in February. They are used in the Battle of the Flowers.

lemons. For Carnaval these citrus fruits are piled up in strange constructions. They are carried on floats that parade through the town streets.

Carnaval in Nice starts with the noise of a cannon firing off a blast from a castle in the city. Hundreds take part in the parades. Floats are all crowded with dancers in beautiful costumes and monsters with papier mâché heads. Women wearing folk dress travel with the floats. Brass bands with tubas, horns, and trumpets play loudly. Crowds line the streets and shower confetti on the floats.

On the very last night of Carnaval there is a fireworks show. The cannon at the castle is fired, and its boom ends the festivities.

On the first day of Lent people go to church. The 40 days of Lenten fasting end with Easter, when the death and resurrection of Jesus is recalled.

9

STES-MARIES-DE-LA-MER

In May a colorful religious festival takes place in the Camargue region of southeast France. Gypsies and other pilgrims come from far and wide to a seaside village where they honor three saints.

For over 400 years Gypsy pilgrims have visited the village of Stes-Maries-de-la-Mer to worship three holy women. In English the village's name means "Saint Marys of the Sea."

The celebrations begin on the evening of May 23 in the Church of Stes-Maries. The church keeps the relics, or bones, of Saint Sarah. The relics of two other women are also kept in the church. They were both called Mary. These three women had all known Jesus and loved Him.

There is a very old story that says four women – *three* Marys and Sarah – came to the Camargue coast after a journey from the far eastern shores of the Mediterranean Sea. Mary Magdalene, one of the women, went to another part of France. Sarah and the other two women, Mary Salomé and Mary Jacobé, brought the teachings of Christ to the Camargue area. The Church of Stes-Maries holds statues of these three women.

The Gypsies claim Sarah is their patron saint – a saint who is special to one group of people. Gypsies are also

Flowers adorn the statues of saints such as Mary Salomé and Mary Jacobé. These women took a long sea journey to France. In memory of their bravery their statues are taken to the sea every year.

called Romanies. They do not settle in one place, but travel about all their lives. Gypsies have roamed Europe and the Middle East for 1,000 years.

Gypsies claim that once, when some of them were in trouble in a strange land, a black woman came to help them. They believe this vision of a woman was Saint Sarah.

GYPSIES

Gypsies speak the Romany language. They came from India. They did not grow crops or have jobs. They were thought of as "wild" people. In the 1930s and 1940s a group called "Nazis" controlled much of Europe. The Nazis tried to get rid of Gypsies and put them in death camps to die. Now there are only about 3 million Gypsies left in the world.

A statue of Sarah, covered with beautiful shawls, is kept in the crypt – an underground room – of the church. Gypsies pin photos of their family to the shawls. They ask the saint to bless those shown in the photos. Hundreds of Gypsies crowd into the crypt, and they pray to Sarah throughout the night.

The next morning a priest leads a Mass,

People pray to the image of Sarah. Candles are placed around the statue. They burn all night.

which is an important Christian religious service. The relics of the saints are shown in the church. People shout, "Long live the Saints." A long line of Gypsies takes Sarah's statue, dressed in lavish lace, to the beach. The Gypsies dance to tambourines and guitars by the sea.

On the morning of May 25 Gypsy men place the statues of the two Marys in a boat, and they carry them down to the beach. A priest follows, leading

For hundreds of years Gypsies lived and traveled in wooden caravans. Nowadays some Gypsies live in motor caravans. Gypsy women are famous for their elaborate folk costumes. They still wear them on special occasions.

hundreds of pilgrims, the religious people who visit holy places.

Cowboys come on their white horses to join the parade. They are from the horse and cattle ranches that are found in the Camargue area. At the beach the boat is placed on the waves. The priest gives his blessing to the sea.

CROQUE MONSIEUR

INGREDIENTS
6 slices white bread
3 T. butter
3 slices American cheese
3 slices ham
Watercress to garnish

Cut the crusts off the bread, then butter the bread on both sides. Make three sandwiches using the ham and cheese. Heat a large frying pan. Melt the remaining butter in the pan, then fry the sandwiches. When the bottom is golden turn with a spatula. Fry on the other side until it is golden too and the cheese has melted. Remove from pan, cut in halves on the diagonal, and serve.

The Gypsies then call out, "Goodbye to the saints," as the holy statues are carried back to church.

The Gypsies also use this time to baptize their children. To "baptize" is to mark a person with water, thus making them a Christian. In the Roman Catholic Church this ritual is usually performed by a priest.

Gypsies also have weddings during this festival. They marry in church following the usual Christian custom, but they also have Romany rituals. The bride and groom make small cuts in their arms. They press the cuts together so that their blood mingles.

In olden days Gypsies danced and played music on village streets and at country fairs. Their music is powerful and rhythmic. The strumming of guitars and the pounding of tambourines fill the air during the festival at Stes-Maries-de-la-Mer.

13

THE SAINT MARYS OF THE SEA

The legend of the Saint Marys of the Sea tells how a band of Christians escaped from Palestine in a small wooden boat. It had neither sails nor oars to move it, yet it crossed the sea. Their journey was a miracle.

IN THE YEARS after Jesus rose to heaven the Christians were busy. They traveled far and wide, saying that Jesus was the Son of God and that God wanted people to give up their old religions to follow Jesus. But this made followers of the Jewish faith want to stop the Christians.

One day a group of Christians was thrown into jail. One of them was Mary Jacobé, sister of the Virgin Mary, Jesus's mother. There was also Mary Salomé, mother of James and John, two of Jesus's disciples. Sarah, their Egyptian servant, was with them. Also traveling with the group was Mary Magdalene, who, according to Christian writings, was the first person to see Jesus after He rose from His Grave. Another of the Christians was Lazarus. Years before Lazarus had died after an illness. Jesus brought him back from the dead and made him alive again. It was a miracle.

The Jewish authorities locked the Christians up in jail for many weeks. Then they dragged the Christians to a beach and forced them to climb into a battered old boat without sails or oars.

Sarah, the servant, wanted to stay with the women. The jailers pushed her away. When the boat containing the Christians washed out to sea, tears

rolled down Sarah's cheeks – she wanted so badly to follow. She decided that her mistresses' God would help her. Sarah threw her veil onto the water, and it turned into a raft. It was another miracle. She paddled out to join the others.

In the boat no one seemed afraid. Mary Jacobé prayed: "Save us, Lord – only to do your work." Another miracle happened. The boat crossed the sea safely and came to the Camargue in France. Mary Jacobé, Mary Salomé, and Sarah stayed in the Camargue. The others traveled throughout Europe. Legend claims the Marys and Sarah brought Christianity to France.

MAKE A TAMBOURINE

Tambourines were played in Ancient Egypt. They are still popular in the Middle East, particularly with performers who dance and sing.

The tambourine is a simple instrument. When it is shaken, the jingles set into its frame make bell-like sounds. It has no pitch, nor can it be played to follow musical notes. The tambourine is important for the noise it brings to the rhythm of the music or the dance. It can be held and played while you are dancing. You can shake the tambourine, or even bang it against your body. Tambourines are often decorated with ribbons. Make your own tambourine. Learn to dance and play.

YOU WILL NEED
Scissors
Sheet of cardboard
Adhesive tape
4 paper clips
6 small bells
Strips of newspaper
All-purpose glue
Acrylic paints
Lengths of narrow ribbon

1 Cut a 2" x 28" strip of cardboard. At 7" intervals cut holes of 1" diameter. Curve strip to form circle and tape ends together. Cut two ½" x 28" strips of cardboard. Tape these to align with inner edges of the circle.

2 Straighten a paper clip. Thread it through two bells. Place over center of a hole. Tape into place. Repeat over two other holes. One hole has no bells.

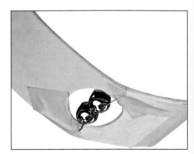

3 Smooth strips of newspaper over inner and outer surface of circle. Apply layers of glue between each strip. Smooth newspaper around holes.

5 Your tambourine is ready to play. Hold it by pushing your thumb through the one hole that does not have bells. Play some music. Follow its rhythm with your tambourine, or simply shake the instrument to make your own beat.

4 When glue covering the newspaper strips dries, apply a layer of white paint over entire surface. Paint design on outer surface of tambourine. When paint is dry, varnish with a thin coat of glue. When this is dry, tie ribbons between bells.

BASTILLE DAY

All over France on July 14 people remember the start of the revolution against the French king Louis XVI and his form of government in 1789. They hold parades and parties to celebrate.

The party starts on the night before Bastille Day, with colorful and exciting fireworks displays. The celebrations go on all night. On Bastille Day itself there are street parties in towns and cities all over France. In Paris there is a grand display of French military power, and the army marches through the streets. There is a spectacular air force flyby. All over the country veterans display their military medals. Veterans are soldiers who have been involved in war. Village people dance in the square, or the village center. All the restaurants offer festive menus.

This day is called Bastille Day because on July 14, 1789, the people

Country musicians favor the accordian. Dances in village squares are often accompanied by this instrument. The French accordian has a series of buttons instead of a keyboard.

of Paris broke into the famous Bastille prison in their city and set the prisoners free.

The attack on the Bastille was the start of a revolt that lasted for many years. Then in 1792 France became a "republic," a country without a king. *"La Marseillaise"* is a song from the revolution. In 1795 French leaders declared that it was the national anthem.

Children of the homeland,
The day of glory has arrived.
Against us is tyranny, with its standard raised.
Can you hear fierce soldiers roaring in our countryside?
They come into our very arms, And kill our sons and friends. Citizens — to arms!
Form into regiments,
let us march! Flood our fields with their blood.

LA MARSEILLAISE

Al - lons, en - fants de la Pa - tri - e, Le jour de gloire est ar - ri - vé. Con - tre nous, de la ty-ran - ni - e L'é -ten dard san - glant est le - vé, L'é - ten - dard — san -glant est le - vé! En - ten - dez - vous, dans les cam - pag - nes Mu - gir ces fa -rou -ches sol -dats? Ils vien-nent jus - ques dans nos bras E-gor-ger vos fils, vos com-pa - gnes. Aux ar - mes, ci - to - yens! For - mez vos ba-tail -lons, Mar - chons, mar - chons! Qu'un sang im - pur A - breu - ve nos sil - lons!

THE ASSUMPTION

The Feast of the Assumption on August 15 honors Mary, the Mother of Jesus. The day has a holiday mood.

For the feast of the Assumption flags and banners are hung from the trees. Long tables are laid out with white cloths. People prefer to eat outdoors on this day.

Before the parties start, Catholics go to Mass and think about the life and purity of the Virgin Mary, the Mother of Jesus.

Mary was a woman who was so good that God chose her to be the mother of Jesus. Christians believe God is the Father of Jesus, and this makes Jesus God as well as man.

It is a Roman Catholic belief that, when the Virgin Mary died, God carried her physical body and

Decorated loaves of bread are prepared for festive feasts and for special occasions.

her spirit up to heaven. This is called the Assumption of Mary. It is a sign of how pure she was that she did not leave her body on Earth. For a long time, even centuries, many ordinary Catholic folk believed in Mary's Assumption. However, the church gave its official blessing to this belief only in 1950.

In 1858 a young girl named Bernadette believed she saw Mary in a grotto, or small cave, at Lourdes, a town in southwestern France. Today there is a shrine marking the spot where the vision appeared. This is the largest shrine to Mary

At Point-Croix, near Douarnenez in Brittany, people hold a religious parade called a "pardon" to mark the day of the Assumption. They dress in folk costumes. In their hands are beautiful banners or statues of Mary, or some may hold lighted candles. They attend a holy Mass specially written for the Virgin Mary.

Catholic clubs or churches that include the word *Mary* in their name also celebrate this Mass to honor the Virgin Mary.

in the world. Lourdes is packed with praying pilgrims, or religious visitors, on the feast day. Masses are said at the grotto and at the basilica, a very large church in Lourdes.

All year pilgrims crowd into Lourdes. Many are crippled or ill, and they believe the waters from a spring near the grotto will heal them.

The font (top) carries images of Jesus, the Son, and Mary, His Mother. The font is a container for water blessed by a priest. Picnics of fruit and cheese are part of the day's pleasures.

MAKE A STAINED GLASS WINDOW

France has many cathedrals that were built in the Middle Ages. Their windows are of stained glass. The most famous are the windows of Chartres Cathedral.

YOU WILL NEED
Tracing paper
Sheet of white paper
Craft glue
Sheet of cardboard, black on one side
Craft knife
Colored tissue paper

The design of our stained glass craft is taken from the fleur-de-lys. This was the proud symbol of the French monarchs, the kings and queens of the country. The fleur-de-lys appeared in their heraldry — their flags of war — and on their crests and rings. You can use a design that has a special meaning for you, your family, or your school.

1 Plan your design before you start. Remember stained glass is held by black lead so plan black outlines. Trace the design onto white paper.

2 Stick designed paper onto cardboard. Stick the paper onto the non-black side. With adult help use the craft knife to cut out the sections where color will be used. Cut through cardboard and paper. These cutouts show black in diagram.

3 Lay your first color sheet of tissue paper over your cutout design. Cut the shape you require. Place to one side. Do this with all the colored sections. Now take one colored cutout section and glue it into place. Repeat with all the colored cutout sections. Remember the black side of the card is on the side you do not glue.

4 As soon as the colored sections are fixed in place, and the glue has dried, turn the design over. The black cardboard has become "leading" around the "glass." You have a fine copy of stained glass. Hang it against a window or place it near a light for a glowing effect.

FÊTE DES REMPARTS

Remparts *means "ramparts," thick walls that fortify old towns. Each September Dinan recalls its medieval past of knights and battles.*

The farmers in Brittany are famous for their goat cheese. They sell produce from the land at the fair. Women may wear simple country clothes to the fair.

Dinan lies on the River Rance in Brittany. Long ago, in 1395, the English were at war with the town. In Brittany at the time lived a famous warrior, Bertrand du Guesclin. He agreed to fight a single battle against Thomas of Canterbury, an English knight. Bertrand won this fierce battle, and the English were forced to leave Dinan. His heart is buried in the town.

Every year this old town holds a big folk festival, "La Fête des Remparts." Certain scenes from medieval life are replayed at the fair. *Medieval* means the "Middle Ages," which were 500 to 700 years ago. The men of Dinan dress themselves as knights, and they stage a "jousting" contest – they ride on horses and hold lances, pole-like sticks. Each rider tries to knock the other one off with

Beef "saucissons" – thick-skinned sausages – come from the local cattle farms.

his lance. Also wearing costumes are jugglers, acrobats, and fire-eaters, all performing at the fair. These acts were part of medieval life. Other people are busy preparing a medieval "banquet," or feast. Farmers set up stalls where they sell jams, ciders, and cheeses. Other stalls display craft products. The festival ends with a display of fireworks.

Knights, the soldiers of medieval times, held jousting tournaments. The warrior knight Bertrand du Guesclin took part in such battles. Jousters at the modern fair enjoy the sport of this old skill.

FRENCH APPLE TART

SERVES EIGHT
1 cup flour
8 T. butter
3 T. cold water
4 apples, peeled and thinly sliced
4 T. sugar
4 T. apricot jelly

To make the crust, cut the butter into the flour with two knives. When it looks like fine cornmeal, mix in the water with a fork. Knead briefly and shape into a ball. Roll out into a circle and fit into a 10-inch quiche pan. The sides should be less than one inch high.

Arrange the apple slices on top of the pastry in the pan in an overlapping circular pattern. Sprinkle with the sugar. Bake for 30 minutes at 350°F. Melt the jelly and brush over the top. Serve warm or cold.

JOAN OF ARC

In the 1400s English armies were trying to capture France. According to legend God inspired Joan, a French girl, to fight back. She became a saint.

SAINT JOAN was told by voices that she had to go to war to save her country, France, from English armies. She thought they were the voices of Saints Michael, Margaret, and Catherine.

She went to see a noble called Baudrimont and told him that God wanted her to save France. Baudrimont saw that Joan would be a good leader, so he sent her to see the French prince, Charles. He thought thieves might attack a woman traveling in the wild countryside so she cut her hair and dressed as a man. Charles knew Joan was coming and wanted to test her. He put on a nobleman's clothes and asked another man to pretend to be prince. But as soon as she walked in, Joan went straight to Charles. She knelt down and told the prince, "God's will is that you are crowned King of France in Rheims."

Charles agreed to let Joan lead an army to Orléans. The English were camped around the city. They would not let any food go into Orléans. They wanted the people to become so hungry that they would give up their city. Joan and her soldiers forced the English to run away. She rode into the city on a white horse, while crowds cheered her arrival. Joan, the girl knight, and her army

went on to win several battles. When it was safe, Charles went to Rheims, and Joan watched proudly as he was crowned King Charles VII of France.

Next, Joan attacked Paris. But she was hurt, and the attack went badly. Later Joan was captured. She was put in jail by the English. They tied her up with chains like a thief.

Angry priests questioned her over and over again. She said that she was told what to do by the voices of saints and angels. After all the questions, the priests said Joan was an heretic, which means someone who goes against Church teaching. In Rouen, on May 30, 1431, the proud girl soldier was tied to a stake and burned to death.

Later the French drove the English out of France. The Catholic Church said Joan was not an heretic. Then, in 1920, it declared that Joan was a saint.

CHRISTMAS

French churches celebrate the birth of Jesus with a service at midnight on the night before Christmas. Afterward people go home and sit down to a big meal called le réveillon.

The feast of *le réveillon*, served at midnight on Christmas Eve, is the main festive meal. Oysters or *foie gras* – a duck liver pâté – often start the meal. This course is followed by roast turkey and chestnuts, or roast goose. In the east of France they eat capon, a type of chicken.

To finish the meal, a Christmas log filled with rich sweet frosting is brought to the table. After the meal people eat *marrons glacés*, that is, candied chestnuts, and chocolate truffles.

The story of the birth of Jesus tells how His mother, Mary, and Joseph, her husband, could not find a place to stay. They stopped in a stable where Jesus was born.

Craftsmen in Provence make santons, *meaning "little saints," from painted clay. Santons are also the people found in nativity scenes.*

French people use clay model figures in "nativity scenes" that show the Holy Family, the stable animals, and the "Three Wise Men," the kings who visited Baby Jesus shortly after His birth.

Nativity sets include figures of local tradesmen. A mother with her baby is part of this scene, too.

Father Christmas, or *Père Noël*, has a busy time. In some areas children expect him to visit on December 6 and on Christmas Eve.

On January 6 France celebrates the Epiphany, the day the Three Kings visited the Baby Jesus.

An almond cake called *galette* is served at Epiphany. A bean, or charm, is hidden inside it. The hostess cuts the cake. The youngest person hides under the table and decides who receives each slice of cake. The person who finds the charm is called the "king" or "queen" for the day and is given a crown. The king or queen is allowed to choose a partner who also has a crown.

Many years ago people burned a large log called the "Yule log" at Christmas. Nowadays the French eat a cake called the bûche de Noël, or "Christmas log."

EASTER

The French island of Corsica lies in the Mediterranean Sea to the south of France. In Sartène on Corsica a man carries a wooden cross through the streets at Easter.

On Good Friday all Christians recall that Jesus died on a wooden cross. The Bible tells us that Jesus carried His cross from Jerusalem to a hill outside the city where He was crucified. Each year on Good Friday in Sartène a man in red robes carries a cross through the streets. A hood covers his face. He is followed by men in black robes chanting a hymn. This procession ends at midnight.

The hooded man is called the "Red Penitent." A penitent is someone who is sorry for doing a bad thing and wants to make up for it. The Easter penitent in Corsica repeats the suffering of Christ as He carried His heavy cross.

WORDS TO KNOW

Crypt: An underground room in a church.

French Revolution of 1789-1799: A period of huge political change during which the monarchy was overthrown, and France became a republic — a form of government in which power is held by the people rather than by kings and queens.

Heretic: A person whose religious beliefs differ from those of the church.

Jousting: A medieval sport in which two men on horseback try to knock each other to the ground using poles called lances.

Mass: A Christian ritual in which bread and wine are used to commemorate the Last Supper of Jesus Christ.

Medieval: To do with the Middle Ages.

Middle Ages: The period between the fifth and the fifteenth centuries.

Patron saint: A saint who is special to a particular group. Many nations, towns, and professions have patron saints.

Penitent: A person who attempts to make amends for his or her sins by performing difficult or painful tasks.

Pilgrim: A person who makes a religious journey, or pilgrimage, to a holy place.

Protestant: A member of one of the Protestant churches, which together form one of the main branches of Christianity. The Protestants split from the Roman Catholic Church in the sixteenth century.

Relic: A part of the body, clothing, or belongings of Jesus or a saint, preserved as a holy item.

Resurrection: The rising of Christ from the dead on Easter Sunday.

Roman Catholic: A member of the Roman Catholic Church, the largest branch of Christianity. The head of this church is the pope.

Saint: A title given to holy people by some Christian churches.

Shrine: A place that is sacred to the memory of a holy person, often housing their relics.

ACKNOWLEDGMENTS

WITH THANKS TO:
Carolyn Manyon. Vale Antiques, London. Elena Paul. Ricki Ostrov. Catholic Truth Society Bookshop, London. Kilburn Accordions, London.

PHOTOGRAPHY:
All photographs by Bruce Mackie except: Marshall Cavendish p. 25, 29. Cover photograph by Katie Vandyk.

ILLUSTRATIONS BY:
Fiona Saunders pp. 4 – 5. Tracy Rich p. 7.
Maps by John Woolford.

Recipes: Ellen Dupont.

SET CONTENTS